Amazing You

Face & Hand Reading

Theresa Cheung

D0818260

a div

Sharp writing for smart people

Welcome to *AMAZING YOU - FACE AND HAND READING*

Find out just how amazing you are by becoming an expert face and hand reader.

Also available are *Astrology, Dreams, Graphology, Numerology, Psychic Powers* and *Spells* – there are more to come in the *Amazing You* series and you can be the first to discover them!

BITE HERE!

Wanna join the gang? All the latest news, gossip and prize giveaways from BITE! **PLUS** more information on new titles in the *Amazing You* series.

Sign up NOW to join the BITE gang, and get a limited edition denim BITE bag or an exclusive preview copy of a brand new teen title, long before it's available in the shops.

To sign up text FACE to 60022

or go to **www.bookswithbite.co.uk**

WIN! How good are your face and hand reading skills? Text FACE and a reading of your favourite celebrity to 60022 and you could win a year's subscription to fab teen magazine *MIZZ* – so get texting now!

Texting costs your normal rate, texts from BITE are free.
You can unsubscribe at any time by texting BITE STOP.
Terms & Conditions Apply. For details go to www.bookswithbite.co.uk

About the series

Amazing You is our stunning new Mind Body Spirit
series. It shows you how to make the most of your life
and boost your chances of success and happiness.
You'll discover some fantastic things about you and
your friends by trying out the great tips and fun
exercises. See for yourself just how amazing you
can be!

Available now
Astrology
Dreams
Face and Hand Reading
Graphology
Numerology
Psychic Powers
Spells

Coming soon
Crystals
Fortune Telling

Acknowledgements

My thanks to the hundreds of children and young adults I've talked to over the years. Your curiosity, freshness and insight were my inspiration while writing this book. A big thank you to my editor Anne Clark for her encouragement and positive energy. Many thanks to everyone at Hodder Children's Books for making this project happen, in particular Katie Sergeant for her help and support. And finally many thanks to my partner Ray and my children, Robert and Ruth, for their love, enthusiasm and patience while I went into exile to complete this project.

About the author

Theresa Cheung was born into a family of psychics, astrologers and numerologists. She gave her first public numerology reading at the age of fourteen, and has been involved in the serious study of the psychic arts for over twenty years. As a former English secondary school teacher and health and fitness instructor Theresa has worked with many young adults. She contributes regularly to women's magazines, such as *Red*, *She* and *Here's Health*, and is the author of over twenty health, popular psychology, humour and New Age books including *Dreams*, *Face and Hand Reading* and *Numerology* in the *Amazing You* series.

Editor: Katie Sergeant
Book design by Don Martin
Cover design: Hodder Children's Books
Diagrams: Lynne Bradley

Published in Great Britain in 2004
by Hodder Children's Books

A catalogue record for this book is available from the British Library.

10 9 8 7 6 5 4 3 2 1

ISBN: 0340882506

Printed and bound by Bookmarque Ltd, Croydon, Surrey

The paper and board used in this paperback by Hodder Children's Books
are natural recyclable products made from wood grown in sustainable
forests. The manufacturing processes conform to the environmental
regulations of the country of origin.

Hodder Children's Books
a division of Hodder Headline Limited
338 Euston Road, London NW1 3BH

Contents

Part three: Making face and hand reading work for you

INTRODUCTION

The power of face and hand reading

Face and hand reading are amazing ways to look into the future. They are age-old sciences that are reliable and a lot easier than you think! No cards, no coins, no charts, no calculations – just a head and a hand and the knowledge in this book.

Your face and hands are full of clues to your character, goals and destiny, and once you begin to read these signs you can take steps to make your life the best that it can be. In this book you'll discover how you can use the technique of reading faces and hands to boost self-confidence, build friendships, resist peer pressure, achieve your goals, and open a whole world of insight into yourself, your friends, your family and your future.

I first started reading faces and hands in my teens, and I've been amazed by how accurate and helpful this art can be. I'm grateful for the many opportunities it has given me over the years and the number of times it has helped me make better decisions. I'm still as enthusiastic about reading hands and faces as I was in my teens, and I hope that you will pick up some of my enjoyment as you read this book.

You can read *Face and Hand Reading* from cover to cover, or you can dip into sections that interest you the most. If you find that two readings contradict each other or you just can't imagine them to be true of you or someone you know, this doesn't mean your reading is incorrect. It  is just indicating possibilities ahead or variations in your character. We can all surprise ourselves at times!

Do remember as you go through the book that ultimately you are in charge of your life. Your face and hands express your potential, but it is up to you to develop them. Face and hand reading do not decide your fate – only you can do that. Who you are can be read on the outside – like the cover of a book – but this is by no means the whole story. So read on to find out just how amazing and unique you really are!

PART ONE

Face reading

CHAPTER ONE

Introduction to face reading

Have you ever judged someone by the look of their face? Our language is full of phrases implying that personality is in the face. 'She has shifty eyes', and 'he has a weak chin, I don't think I can trust him', are just two of the many examples. Without knowing it, we make so many assumptions about someone's character by their physical appearance. In the art of face reading we learn why. Each feature of line and shape has a meaning that indicates our character, relationships and destiny.

Face reading has been practised for centuries. The earliest records date back to China, two hundred years before Christ. Over

thousands of years, the Chinese developed one of the most complete systems for reading fortunes in people's faces that exists anywhere. Chinese emperors, rulers and teachers have used this method for centuries to understand a person's nature and future. Now you can do the same.

When you learn face-reading techniques you'll discover things about your face and the faces of your friends and family that you never noticed before, like eyebrow shape, ear position or nostril size. So it might be a good idea to keep a mirror by your side while you read this section. Finding out new things about your face and yourself is part of the fun of face reading.

Face reading can not only help you understand and deal with others better, but it can also help build up your self-esteem. How you view your face is often connected to your opinion of the rest of you. You'll discover that every detail about your face means something wonderful – from the shape of your cheeks to the position of your eyes. You'll begin to appreciate just how unique and wonderful you are.

✳   ★   ★   ★

I've always hated my nose. The way it looks, and the fact that it's so big. When I was little I'd do drawings of smiling faces with no noses. My parents and teachers would always remind me to draw the nose, but I never did. The way I see my nose has changed since I started face reading. If only I'd known sooner that having a long nose is pretty cool.

Sarah, 12

I've got this really, really high forehead. I've always wanted to grow out my fringe but felt too embarrassed. When I found out that having a high forehead means I'm highly imaginative and creative I decided to take the plunge. I love my new look!

Jane, 15

I've always envied people with neat little ears because my ears are big and they stick out. I used to get teased all the time. Face reading has shown me that there is a lot to like about my ears. Almost as soon as I stopped feeling ashamed of them, the teasing stopped. I think people sensed the change in me – I felt more confident and sure of myself.

Chloe, 15

Face reading will help you to focus on the positive features of your face that you may never have noticed before. Learning to love your face and be happy with the way you look is a crucial step towards happiness and self-belief. If you're not yet convinced, just read on to find out how ...

CHAPTER TWO

How to see like a face reader

Within seconds of seeing a face, you notice if it's male or female; young or old. The next thing you notice relates to attractiveness. Psychological research says that most people seek boy and girl friends who are similar to them in the looks department – so if you rate yourself as 10/10 you probably won't fancy someone you consider to be 4/10. Much of what we like or dislike when meeting someone really comes down to 'cuteness' screening. So when you begin to face read, keep this in mind: face reading is about *studying* a person's face. It's got nothing to do with assessing how attractive you think a person is.

Also watch out for confusing a person's 'look' with their face. We are often mesmerized by a person's look –

their hairstyle, make-up and clothes – but a person's look won't reveal their personality as much as their face can. Facial features can't be faked, so face reading gives you more accurate information.

✷✶ FACE FABLES

Here's a quick 'true or false?' quiz to help you think about what it means to be a face reader.

1. Someone with beady eyes is untrustworthy.

2. Don't trust anyone who won't look you in the eye.

3. People with full lips are sexy.

4. Intelligence shows in the shape of the skull – big head, big brains.

5. Most people don't like their chins.

6. Watching someone's expression helps to put you in control.

7. People from the same ethnic group all look very similar.

8. The eyes are the mirror of the soul.

✦ 1. False. What are beady eyes anyway? Do you
think of close-set eyes, deep-set eyes or small
eyes? When you learn to interpret these traits
you'll discover their meanings, which are probably
not what you expect.

✦ 2. False. Unwillingness to look someone in the eye
is not a clue to honesty. It could be a clue to
shyness or depression. And in certain cultures
around the world, eye contact is avoided as a
mark of respect.

✦ 3. False. Anyone can be sexy. For every sexy
celebrity who has full lips, there is a sexy celebrity
with thinner lips. Think Avril Lavigne
and Justin Timberlake. Here's a more
reliable way to read lips: lip fullness
relates to self-disclosure. The fuller the lips, the
more likely someone is to share personal
information about themselves.

✦ 4. False. The front of a person's face tells you a
lot more about them than the back of their head.
Phrenology, which gauged IQ by skull size, was
often used in the past to brand people good, bad
or insane, and its accuracy has long since been
discredited. Face reading adds depth to your

understanding of others, and it has nothing to do with superstition or phrenology.

✧ 5. False. According to surveys, most people dislike their noses more than their chins. When you start to learn the inner meaning of face traits you'll learn a new respect for your features – including your chin and your nose.

✧ 6. False. Paying attention to expression is more likely to mislead you. Remember moods can change and are often incomplete. It is far better to read faces for features, lines and shapes.

✧ 7. False. Ethnic similarities are not a significant part of face reading. When you learn to read faces properly, people are impossible to stereotype and are completely individual.

✧ 8. False. Soul stuff is visible, but usually it's in the form of emotion, and emotions can change. For face readers, the entire face mirrors the soul.

✶✶ LEVEL WITH YOUR FACE

Never bend your head. Always hold it high.
Look the world straight in the eye.
Helen Keller (1880-1968)

As you get ready to read your face, look at it from a straight angle. Don't look up or down. To see the truth, you need to be on the level. The same applies when you read other people.

Reading faces takes time. A quick glance isn't enough. You need to really look at all the features one at a time. This is because each feature means something. As with anything, the more you practise, the better you will get.

And finally, when you do face read, don't judge or condemn what you see. Try to look at a face – your own or someone else's – with the intention of showing a genuine interest and respect. When you sincerely want to get to know someone better, this tends to invite other people to do the same to you. Don't you respond differently when people show genuine interest in you as a person?

✦✦ AM I TOO YOUNG TO READ FACES?

Although it does take until you are about eighteen for your features to finally settle, there is no reason why you can't use face-reading techniques to learn more about yourself and your friends. Just bear in mind that what you see now will almost certainly change in the next few years and you will need to constantly update your interpretations. Part of growing up is learning about yourself and exploring different aspects of your personality. Face reading can draw your attention to these different aspects.

Why not have some fun reading adults? Focus on your parents, teachers and other authority figures. They play such an important part in your life and face reading is a great way to gain more information about them.

CHAPTER THREE

Face types

 Face reading is based on the principles of the five Chinese elements: wood, fire, metal, earth and water. The shape of your face and your features determine which type you are, and this can then tell you a lot about your health and your personality.

To find your element, make a note of the answers that most correspond to your face shape and personality traits. Although you may find that you can be a mix, you are likely to find one type that fits you more than others.

The basic shape
A 1 have a long face and nose with a broad, high forehead.

B I have a long face with narrow and prominent cheekbones.

C I have a short, square face with a prominent jaw.

D I have an oval face with high, wide cheekbones.

E I have a round, soft full face.

A little more detail

A I have narrow cheeks and large eyes.

B I have pointed features, dry skin and freckles.

C I have a sallow complexion and heavy eyebrows.

D I have a naturally pale complexion, prominent arched eyebrows and straight hair.

E My large eyes are my most noticeable feature.

Positive qualities

A I'm a leader and I love challenges.

B I'm enthusiastic, adventurous and love taking risks.

C I'm practical, reliable and sensible.

D I'm strong-willed, happy to give advice and like to solve my own problems.

E I'm quiet, sensitive and a good listener.

And the negative

A I can be rash, impulsive and impatient.

B I can be erratic, moody and scatty.

C I can be cynical, suspicious and critical.

D I can be inflexible and feel isolated at times.

E I tend to feel insecure and I worry a lot.

 Which celebrity does your face shape most resemble?

A Kim Cattrall

B Madonna

C Jennifer Aniston or Elizabeth Hurley

D Gwyneth Paltrow or Cate Blanchett

E Nicole Kidman

Mostly As: Wood

Full of fun, vitality, humour and insight, you are passionate, forward-thinking, lively and outgoing and definitely the person to know at school. However, you can be irritable and impatient at times. You are the type of person who needs goals and activities. The wood element is related to anger, but this isn't necessarily a bad thing as it can give you the energy and drive you need to achieve your aims. The downside is that when you can't get what you want you can get moody and aggressive.

Mostly Bs: Fire

You are courageous, strong, adventurous and determined. You are active and love the outdoors, and can be relied upon to get the party started. But when your fire goes out you can be withdrawn and lack motivation. You need to find happiness within yourself instead of seeking it through activities or your friends. Getting up early in the morning for school isn't easy for you, and you tend to be more creative in the evenings and well into the night.

Mostly Cs: Earth

You are trustworthy, straightforward and reliable, but you don't like it if friends and family place too many demands on you. You work hard at school, but you do tend to worry a lot and can be prone to dithering. The emotion of sympathy is related to Earth, so you may be very caring when a friend or relative is in need of some TLC. You are good at taking care of others, but sometimes neglect your own needs. It's important that you take care of yourself too.

Mostly Ds: Metal

This is the element of the mind, and you are very strong-willed, broad-minded, rational, intellectual and focused. You enjoy the challenge of school, probably more than any other type. Sometimes, though, you can pay too much attention to the details and lose sight of the bigger picture. At your best you have a great sense of humour and are hardworking. But if you are out of sorts you can become very negative.

Mostly Es: Water

You are creative and very active, but you can be rash and impatient at times. You can be outgoing and social but also quiet and gentle. You are a good communicator and are easily swayed when a friend in need appeals to your emotions. There is a vitality about you that attracts others, and you are likely to be surrounded by friends. You are good at getting things done and motivating other people. You tend to have more stamina in the morning.

 In Part three you'll discover how knowing your face type can help you support your health and well-being, but for now just take the time to appreciate your own face type. What can you learn about yourself? Have fun discovering which face type your friends, family and teachers are. Think about how knowing this can help you understand and relate to them better.

CHAPTER FOUR

Face facts: eyes, noses and cheeks

The five features of Chinese face reading are the eyes, eyebrows, mouth, ears and nose. Also significant are the forehead, chin and cheeks. Let's see what they have to say about you and the people in your life. In Part three we'll explore how this information can help you in your daily life.

Eyes

Most of the time the eyes win our attention. Yet often the way we look at eyes stops us from really understanding them. How about the insight we could gain if we gazed not in them but around them? The eyelids, for example, or the structure or position of eyes can tell us a great deal about different aspects of ourselves.

Lower eyelid

When you feel emotional, vulnerable and/or infatuated, the lower eyelid tends to curve, giving the eyes a rounded shape. Try it and see. Imagine the boy you fancy is about to make a move, and then glance at your expression in the mirror. By contrast, when you feel hurt, suspicious or shy the lower eyelid tends to narrow. Again check this out. Imagine that your best friend has been gossiping behind your back and you are about to confront her. Now take a look at your expression in the mirror.

Your lower eyelid also has a default setting, and that's what you need to look at now. How

curved are your lower eyelids when you are at rest? If they are very curved, you have a vulnerable and open nature and can be easily hurt by others. The straighter your lower eyelids, the less willing you are to open up to people until you know them really well. If your eyelid curve is moderate you have struck a balance

– closing yourself off a little when you meet new people but remaining open enough to let through the friends you need.

How close are your eyes to each other?

Close-set eyes live like neighbours on either side of the nose. Far-set eyes space themselves far apart. If you have close-set eyes, you have a talent for focusing. Nothing and nobody escapes you, and you excel in anything that requires intensity and concentration. Think David Beckham or Christina Aguilera. People with far-set eyes have a knack for coming up with great ideas and leading by example. Imaginative and quick to take the lead, they are often dreamy and ahead of their time. Think Cameron Diaz, Beyoncé and Justin Timberlake.

✦ ✦ EYE POINTERS TO LOOK OUT FOR

* Large, wide-open eyes are an indication of an easygoing, friendly person.
* Eyes that are bright and well-shaped but watery suggest sex appeal.
* Long and bow-shaped eyes suggest a creative, sympathetic but cautious nature. The longer and smaller the eye, the greater the tendency to be a loner.

* If your eyes tilt up on the side of the face, you are more likely to be optimistic, even idealistic. If they tilt down, you tend to be a problem solver. And if your eye angle is even, you are neither a pessimist nor an optimist but a realist.
* If your face remains level but your eyes dart back and forth, this suggests that your head is full of ideas, plans and schemes.
* If your eyes slowly wander when you are speaking, you plan carefully but can be unreliable at times.
* If eyes rise upwards this is a sign of confidence.

* A constant gaze suggests an honest, reliable character.
* Want to know if someone is truly pleased to see you or just faking a smile? Watch their eyes. When a person is really pleased and the smile is genuine you'll notice that their eyebrows lower a little and tiny creases appear on the side of the eye. When the smile isn't real you won't notice any of the above.

***

Noses

Hopefully this section will give you reasons to love your nose, whatever it looks like.

Do you have a short nose, a long nose or an average-length nose? If your nose is short you have a wonderful talent for hard work and getting things done. You are highly motivated, and need to find ways to use your considerable talents. If your nose is long, you have a gift for creativity and planning ahead. And if your nose is moderate length, you are flexible and have the best of both worlds, combining motivation with creativity to get the job done.

Now let's take a look at your nose in profile, or sideways on. If yours is straight, you are organized, hardworking and one of life's high flyers. If your nose is scooped and curves slightly inwards and upwards, you are highly intuitive and it's important that you listen to your feelings and follow your heart. And finally, if your nose is

arched – the tip curves downwards – you have a talent for working creatively. This doesn't mean other shaped noses aren't creative, it's just that if you have an arched nose you *need* to be creative.

Now let's check out your nostril size. Looking at your nose from the front, are your nostrils large or small? If you can see the whole shape, count them as large. If they are large you are someone who likes to live and spend in a big way – either buying lots of stuff for yourself or doing huge things for others. If your nostrils are small it doesn't mean you aren't generous, it just means that you are likely to be less impulsive and to think more carefully before committing yourself.

So you see, noses have so much to tell you. They can be particularly helpful, as you'll find out in Part three, when making decisions about work and money and even when choosing a date. But now we'll turn to the face part that tells us about your power for getting your way with others – your cheeks.

Cheeks

How prominent are your cheeks? Do they grab your attention? Or are you forever applying blusher to accentuate them?

If your cheeks are prominent, this goes with the kind of person who likes to stand out in the crowd. Lots of performers and celebrities, such as Britney Spears and Kate Winslet, have prominent cheeks. If you have less prominent cheeks, your style is more subtle. You prefer to ask other people for their opinions and advice. You are thoughtful and considerate, and the shape of your cheeks encourages other people to trust you and warm to you.

How high are your cheekbones? If they are right beneath your eye sockets, they are high and you are likely to have an iron will and fight for what you believe in. If your cheekbones are lower,

23

it means that you are more flexible, tolerant and open minded.

And finally, do your cheeks thin out below your cheekbones? If they do, you have an advantage when it comes to making a good first impression. People who have this trait are often considered natural leaders. If your cheekbones are not so pronounced and your face gets wider below them, you are a good listener and people come to you with their problems because they know you can handle it. If your forehead is wider than your cheeks, however, you are intense, passionate and idealistic and you can accomplish a great deal. Just watch out that you don't exhaust yourself! Those with even features, by contrast, are less likely to crave the limelight but more liable to achieve results.

So, as you can see, every face type has its special qualities. It doesn't matter whether your nose is short or long, or your cheeks high, or your forehead broad, you have all the talents you need to live a happy and successful life. Start making a list of all the positive qualities associated with your face type, and celebrate the wonderful person you are!

CHAPTER FIVE

Face facts: the rest of your face

Let's move on to the next features face readers consider important: eyebrows, ears, lips, teeth and chins.

Eyebrows

One minute of eyebrow reading can tell an experienced face reader as much about a person as an hour of small talk. In general, eyebrows tell us how creative you are and how you think and talk.

Look first at where the hair appears in your eyebrows. If there's a lot of it at the inner eyebrow points, near the nose, but then it fades away at the outer points, you are creative and full of ideas but sometimes lack the discipline to follow through. If your eyebrows get stronger at the ends, then you have a talent for details and seeing things through to the end. If your eyebrow hair distribution is even throughout you have a nice balance between creative drive and attention to detail.

Typically, lots of eyebrow hair suggests the ability to multitask and a magical kind of intelligence – think about pictures you have seen of Einstein. Thin eyebrows, by contrast, go with mental intensity. You are no less intelligent than your thicker-browed friends but it's best for you to stick to one task at a time.

If your eyebrow is nicely curved, this suggests that you are very sensitive to the feelings of others. The more curved the eyebrow, the more emotionally vulnerable you can be. Paul McCartney has very curved eyebrows, and more than any other Beatle he has specialized in writing love songs. Straight eyebrows suggest a passion for logic – it's no accident that Mr Spock from *Star Trek* has ruler-straight brows. And finally, eyebrows that contain a hinge, where the hair changes direction

– Kylie Minogue is a good example – suggest detachment and a seductive, at times, what's-in-it-for-me attitude.

Should I pluck my eyebrow hair?

Wild and scattered eyebrow hair suggests wild ideas, which can result in outrageous creativity, as in the case of Einstein, or Warren Buffet, who has been named the richest person in America. You might want to tame those hairs with some gentle tweaking, but don't lose them completely. Pluck them only if they grow together in the middle, for when eyebrows merge into one this suggests nonstop thinking and a mind that can't switch off.

✦✦✦

Ears

An old Chinese proverb says that since the ear is the only feature that cannot move, it cannot lie. The ears are just as important when face reading as the other features of the face.

Look at your ears in a mirror, and compare their length to the length of your face from forehead to chin. How many ears could you line up, end to end, before running out of face space? If you can line up only three or four, then you have long ear length. If you can line up seven or more, you have short ear length, and anything in between is medium.

So, what difference does length of ears make? Generally, the longer the ears, the greater the ability to listen. People with shorter ears listen only to what matters to them. As for medium ears, you are flexible in the listening department. Sometimes you'll take in everything, other times you'll switch off.

Another thing to look out for is how close the ears are to your head. Generally, the closer they are, the more your need to belong. You are very tactful and have the ability to fit into any social situation. The more your ears angle out from your face, the more likely you are to want to defy convention. The author J. M. Barrie's ears stood out from his head and he is renowned for creating Peter Pan, the boy who refused to grow up and conform to the adult world. If your ears fit into neither category, conformity isn't an issue for you, but you might sometimes lack tolerance for those around you.

Read my lips

Your mouth is a good indicator of your character and the way you express yourself. Examine your mouth when it is not speaking or smiling and is just at rest. Does your mouth lift at the corner, does it angle downward, or is it straight? Mouth angle tells you how you interpret what other people are saying. If your mouth is straight, you'll hear the facts; if it angles up you'll think positively; if it angles down you could have a tendency to brood. But don't overlook the strength of a downward-angling mouth, which is being sensitive and kind to the feelings of others.

Full lips are all the rage in Hollywood now, but what do they mean in face reading? Generally the fuller the lips, the more likely you are to enjoy talking and opening up to others. People with thinner lips find it harder to talk about personal things. If your lower lip is very full, then you can be very seductive and persuasive – think Elvis Presley. If your upper lip is fuller, then you like to speak your mind and shake people up with outrageous truths.

Now let's check out your mouth length. Are your lips short, long or medium? Generally the shorter the lips, the more you prefer to communicate on a one-to-one basis. Long lips go with the ability to talk to anyone. Friendliness is another name for this gift. Julia Roberts is a spectacular example of the appeal of long lips that reach out to millions of people. And don't underestimate the value of traits in the medium range. If your lips are medium length, you are flexible. You feel equally comfortable talking to one person as you do to a larger audience, and your open communication style makes life much easier for you.

⋆⋆ SPECIAL LIPS!

Long, thin lips
This mouth can talk to anyone about anything – you have a millionaire mouth if you use it wisely.

Long, full lips
You are a born talker and have a wacky sense of humour – think Eddie Murphy.

Short, thin lips
You have powerful lips and your words carry great power – think Bob Dylan and designer Giorgio Armani.

Short, full lips
These lips are best-friend lips, and they suggest a willingness to reveal all. Just one catch though – they prefer one-to-one. Think Richard Gere and Brad Pitt.

Teeth

Teeth, in general, indicate the ability to make decisions in life and how well you learn from your mistakes. The front teeth symbolize the size of a person's ego. Basically, the larger they are in comparison to your other teeth, the bigger the ego! Small front teeth suggest humility, selflessness and a concern for others. Mother Teresa is a classic example.

Your canines (teeth on either side of the front four) often indicate aggression, and a prominent, pointy pair suggest a killer instinct. This isn't a bad trait to have if used wisely, but it can be scary to other people. Finally, if your upper teeth stick out further than your lower teeth, you tend to bend yourself backwards to please others; while those whose lower teeth stick out more tend to be tireless fighters. If both sets of teeth are even, lucky you! This goes with a rare form of inner balance.

Few of us have perfect teeth. You can envy another person's set all you like, but the fact remains that each type of teeth and mouth has its own positive qualities. What are yours?

The priority areas

The proportions of your face between your forehead, nose and chin can tell you lots about where your priorities lie. The first priority area is the forehead. The second priority area stretches from your eyebrows to the lowest part of your nose; and the third stretches from the lowest part of your nose to the bottom of your chin.

If your forehead area is larger than the other two areas, then you are into thinking. You love philosophy, teaching and writing. Ideas and imagination inspire you. If your nose area is the largest, you are a go-getter and very ambitious. If the chin area is the largest, you are practical, down-to-earth and incredibly sexy. And if all three areas are equal, lucky you! You tend to lead a very calm and balanced life. You'll probably find that two areas are larger than the other. If that's the case, think about the information above and consider the possibilities.

33

Priority areas can be very helpful when it comes to compatibility, especially in relationships and friendships. But more on this later!

Jaws and chins

Your jaw and chin can reveal vital secrets about how you act in the world. With few exceptions, wide jaws suggest strength and sexiness in both men and women. You are the type to never give in and hang on at all costs. If your jaws are narrow, you are stronger in a different way and sometimes have the advantage because you can resolve problems without resorting to conflict. And if you have average jaw length you have the best of both worlds. You handle conflict well but also know when it is time to move on.

How about chins? It's common knowledge that chins that jut out, like Drew Barrymore's, relate to competitiveness. But the danger here is unnecessary aggressiveness. A receding chin, by contrast, shows community spirit. Rather than tearing relationships

apart through conflict, these
people prefer to compromise and
work together. Their challenge is to
gain the respect of others in a world that doesn't
always value public spirit. As for even-angled
chins, they indicate a mixture of compromise and
aggression. These people won't take advantage,
but they won't get trampled on either.

Does your chin look long or short when you
look at it in the mirror from the side? Chin length
relates to risk taking, and your ability to bounce
back from setbacks. A long chin means that you
can 'take it on the chin' when setbacks and
disappointments happen and come out stronger.
What about a short chin? Does it deserve to be
called weak? Not really. Although the short chin
suggests someone who is less willing to take
physical risks, it does show a readiness to
take emotional risks. Unfortunately, it might
also indicate a tendency to feel guilty and to
be overly sensitive to criticism.

How about chin width? Narrow chins suggest
that when the going gets tough you prefer to go
it alone, or with just a few close friends. Wider
chins suggest you have a big support group and

you expect plenty of help to achieve your goals.

And finally, the outline of your chin at the bottom of your face can be significant. If it's curved, you are likely to be humanitarian and hospitable. If it's straight, you are likely to make choices based on ideas rather than people. You'll show your mettle in political rallies and other cause-related events. If your chin is angled, there is a need to stay in control and often an iron will to go with it. Nobody messes with you!

By now you should be becoming familiar with what different areas of your face signify. You will be well acquainted with your own face and can see the potential in your features. As you learn more about face reading you'll uncover this exciting way to find out more about yourself and other people. So keep reading to progress to the next stage – facial mysteries.

CHAPTER SIX

Facial mysteries

Now that we've begun to explore facial features –
eyebrows, ears, eyes, cheeks, nose and chin – you
are no longer a novice face reader. Is information
starting to come to you from unexpected face
parts? It's now time to introduce you to the world
of lopsidedness. Yes, most of us are lopsided, and
there is nothing bad about it at all. It's
fascinating, revealing and very human.

Look in a mirror and cover one side of
your face with a piece of paper. Now move the
paper to cover the other side. The sides are so
different you could almost be looking at two
different people!

The right side of your face represents the first impression you give to others. The left side reveals your private self, and how you function with friends and family.

If you are starting to feel overwhelmed with all this information, give yourself time. Slow down enough to look at one feature at a time. Then when you feel ready, add depth to your reading by taking account of the two different sides of a person's face.

Shapes

As we've run through the different facial features, have you noticed that a certain shape suggests a certain meaning? Curved tends to suggest people-orientated; straight idea-orientated; and angled control-orientated. So if you see a curved chin and curved eyebrows, this is someone who puts people first, whereas someone with straight eyebrows and a straight chin is thoughtful and logical. But what if there is a mix, say, curved eyebrows and a straight chin? Eyebrows, you remember, tell us how people think, but chins tell us how they act, so this person notices feelings, but they act according to their principles.

Don't be surprised if what you learn from a face appears contradictory. We are all a mass of ideas and endless possibilities. Feelings often conflict with ideals and vice versa. Your skill as a face reader is to unravel the mystery behind the face, to find the strengths and weaknesses of each feature and then see how it all merges into the bigger picture. What story does the person you are reading reveal? What insight does it give you about their struggles, their hopes, their fears and their dreams?

★★ FAMOUS FACES

Before reading your friends and family, have some fun and put all that we have learnt into practice with some celebrity face reading. Grab a magazine, cut out some celebrity photos and take time to study their features. What story

does their face tell? Here we look at Britney
Spears and Victoria Beckham to get you thinking
along the right lines.

Britney Spears possesses classic traits
of beauty and sexiness, which exude from
her face. Her wide-open expressive eyes
radiate a bewitching self-assurance and
are facial indicators of her success and popularity.
Her shining, attractively dome-shaped forehead
tells us she is idealistic and imaginative. Her high
forehead also suggests that Britney demands
intelligence in her friends and boyfriend, and her
slightly elongated eyes show that she can lose
interest quickly if her desires aren't satisfied. Her
cheeks are full and rosy, and these also add
weight to the fact that she loves to be the centre
of attention. Her nostrils are not
too visible, and this shows that
she is good with money and will
probably always have plenty of
it. Her chin and jaw are in proportion, which
indicates a tenacious and energetic personality –
this is especially evident in her charismatic
performances.

Victoria Beckham's high forehead also indicates brightness, and the intensity and drawing power in Victoria's eyes suggest a defiant attitude. Victoria's  long nose shows her need to be creative and her love of friends and admirers. Her V-shaped eyebrows are precise and show determination, persistence and an ability to get things done. Because they are set low upon her eyes, there is an impulsive streak, which means that she is more likely to speak before she thinks. The sensual side of her nature is indicated by her

 lips – she has a philtrum, or vertical groove, in her upper lip (we'll talk more about that in Part three) – but those lips also exhibit a slight downward turn at the edges. This is the mark of a person who does not hesitate to make her desires and her displeasure known very quickly.

As you study famous faces or the faces of great artists or sports figures, don't be surprised if you find a bit of yourself in them. You may have always thought of yourself as kind of average, but hopefully face reading will show you how beautifully individual you are and help you appreciate your uniqueness and beauty in all its depth and detail.

PART TWO

Hand reading

CHAPTER SEVEN

Introduction to hand reading

Since the beginning of time people have been fascinated by hands. The earliest palm imprints came from the Stone Age, so from very early on people knew just how important hands are. Modern science shows us that there is more brain activity related to our hands than to any other organ in the human body.

At some point in time people began to see that every hand was different, and from that discovery, palmistry, or the art of hand reading, was born.

Palmistry is thought to have originated in ancient China around 3000 BC, while evidence of the practice can also be found in ancient Indian scriptures. The ancient Egyptians were probably students of the art, and they most likely passed it on to the Greeks. Some 2,300 years ago Aristotle, a famous Greek philosopher, wrote a book on palmistry for Alexander the Great, and the basic principles outlined there haven't changed much over the years. Palmistry spread to Europe in the early fourteenth century, but it wasn't until the nineteenth century that it began to be treated as an accurate science. Until then, most people believed you had to be psychic to read palms.

Palmistry is an excellent tool for revealing character and information about a person's health. By learning how to read the secrets of your hands, you will become part of a tradition that has lasted for centuries and is still very much alive today.

Hand reading is also a wonderful way to make new friends and impress that boy you've got your eye on. There is nothing more inviting and exciting for other people than a private palm reading. Do remember, though, as you learn this new skill that palmistry can suggest possible outcomes to situations, but it doesn't decide your fate. Only you can do that. Palmistry can help encourage and motivate you to reach your potential and be the best you can be, but it can't make those changes for you. It is you who has the power to make decisions. And when you grow and change, the lines on the palm of your hands change too. That's why you should do a reading every few months.

A complete hand reading not only takes into account the lines of the hand but also its shape, texture and suppleness, as well as finger formation. In this section you'll find a beginner's guide to reading your palm. Use it in conjunction with the accompanying diagrams and also with the information in Part three. There we will put everything together and see just how helpful palmistry can be in your daily life.

* * * * * *

I love to palm read for my friends. It's really exciting for them, and it helps me because I get to learn extra things about them.
  Melanie, 12

* * *

It's funny because you think you know people really well, but we actually don't take in that much detail about their hands and faces as we are so used to seeing them every day. I've definitely seen my friends and family in a new light!

Priti, 16

✳ CHAPTER EIGHT

The whole hand

Start by identifying your dominant and
nondominant hands. If you're right-handed, then
your right hand is the dominant one.
If you're left-handed, your left hand
is dominant. Your dominant
hand can tell you about your
present – what you are actually doing. Your
nondominant hand tells you what you were
born with – it's a bit like a map of your potential.
As you're starting out, I suggest that you focus
your attention on the dominant hand only. Let's
take a look at the different features of your hands
and see what they reveal about you.

Handshake

You can tell a lot about someone simply by shaking their hand. Someone who grips your hand

firmly is likely to give a better impression than someone who offers a weak and lifeless grip. Something to bear in mind next time you are introduced to someone you need to impress!

If someone offers you their hand in a handshake and all the fingers touch, this person will be wary, cautious and lacking in confidence. If the fingers are widely spread the person is likely to be outgoing, enthusiastic and has nothing to hide. This person will be more confident and self-assured than someone who holds their hands with fingers touching.

Consistency and flexibility

How flexible or bendy are your hands? If they are flexible, you are more likely to be adaptable and easygoing than people with more rigid hands. Now press gently on your palms. People with soft and spongy hands tend to be pleasure seekers who love to daydream and take life easy. People with firmer, stronger palms are more resilient and love the challenge of hard work.

Texture

How do your hands feel to touch? If they are smooth this can suggest that you take good care of yourself and may be reluctant to get your hands dirty or fully commit to situations or relationships. If your hands are rough this can suggest that you are willing to work hard, get involved and take responsibility.

Size

Generally the larger the hands, the more a person enjoys working with intricate detailed things. People with small hands want to skip the detail and undertake big projects.

Square or oblong?

If your palm is square shaped, you are more likely to be down-to-earth and practical. You have loads of stamina and energy and are a hard worker.

If your palm is oblong, you are creative, gentle and idealistic, but you may have a tendency to daydream.

Finger length

How long or short are your fingers in proportion to your palm? If you aren't sure, they are probably medium in length.

If you've got short fingers, you like to get things done quickly and efficiently. You like being busy and can do a number of things at once. You like starting new things but are not always so good at finishing them, as you get bored with the details. People with long fingers, by contrast, enjoy work that is detailed. They are patient and like to take their time, and they love to finish what they start. If you've got medium fingers, you are a mixture of the two. You can be patient at times but also lose interest.

Knowledge about finger length can be quite useful. If you are standing in a queue, choose a line with a short-fingered cashier, who is more likely to move quickly than one who is long fingered and likes to check every detail.

Left-handedness

Approximately one in ten people are left-handed, and studies show that left-handed children are likely to be very creative and have extremely high verbal or mathematical ability. There are more left-handed men than women in the world, and no-one knows why. Famous left-handers include Prince Charles and John McEnroe.

Hand classification

Now that we have discussed hand and finger type, we can begin to classify hands. Which of the following is most suited to you?

Square hand with short fingers (Earth hand)

You take life as it comes and love the outdoors. You are always busy and enjoy doing things with your hands. You are practical, reliable and dependable although you can be impatient and critical at times.

Square palm with long fingers (Air hand)

Intellectual, intuitive and expressive, you are easy
to get along with. You are interested in
travel, freedom and anything that is out of
the ordinary. You are practical, good with
particulars and you need constant challenges.

Oblong palm with short fingers (Fire hand)

Imaginative, enthusiastic, versatile and
impatient, you are full of ideas but
they are not always realistic. You
need constant challenges but can get
frustrated with the nitty-gritty and often lose
interest before the task is complete. You are
generous, sociable, energetic and exciting, but
your changeable nature can be frustrating
for others.

Oblong palm with long fingers (Water hand)

Extremely imaginative, sensitive and idealistic, you
give the impression of being calm and in control,
but you often suffer from nerves and tension.

This is the hand shape of the artist, who may not be overly practical in daily life.

✦✦ HAND GESTURES

Do you use your hands a lot when you speak? Many of us do and, according to psychologists, it suggests that our brains are trying to make sense of things and get to the truth. In fact, one of the first things to look for to see if a friend isn't telling the truth is the amount of hand gestures they are using. Most of the time there is less or no hand movement at all when someone is lying.

So that's an introduction to the whole hand – its proportions and what they tell you about yourself. Now you're ready to move on to the next chapter in hand reading – the fingers, thumbs and mounts. Read on to find out more!

CHAPTER NINE

Fingers, thumbs and mounts

We've seen how long fingers can suggest patience and attention to detail, while short fingers suggest a faster, more concise approach. We've also seen how someone who holds their hand out with fingers held apart will be more open and confident than someone whose fingers are pressed together. But what else can fingers tell us?

The colour of fingernails can give a clue to the person's health. The ideal nail should be pinkish in colour and contain no ridges or white spots. White dots are causes by stress and anxiety, and they can also indicate a calcium deficiency. If the nail is white, it can suggest iron deficiency, and if it is red it belongs to people who get overexcited quickly. Check out yours to see how

healthy you are! The ideal fingernail is
also slightly longer than it is wide, and
people with these nails are faithful,
honest and energetic. People with very
long fingernails are sensitive and emotional but
often rather selfish. People with short fingernails
are hard on themselves and overly critical.

Scientists have discovered that the length of
someone's fingers can be a strong indicator of
how attractive they are to the opposite sex.
It seems that the longer a boy's ring finger (third
 finger) compared to the index finger (first
finger) the more likely he is to consider
himself unattractive, and the longer a girl's
index finger compared with the ring finger
the less likely she is to see herself as
appealing. Don't panic though if you find that
your ring or index finger is too long;
this doesn't mean you aren't attractive,
it means that you don't *think* of yourself
as attractive. Work on your self-esteem.
Everyone is beautiful in their own way.
There is so much about you that is fascinating
and amazing – you just need to believe in it
and let other people see it.

Here's a diagram showing the four fingers and what they are called:

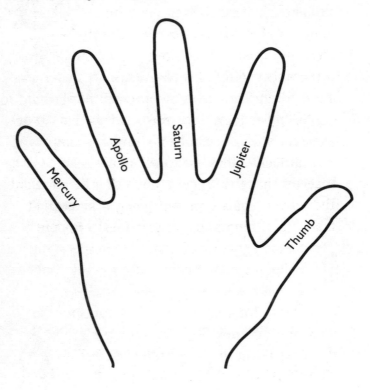

First finger (Jupiter finger)

The first finger, or index finger, is called the Jupiter finger, and it suggests your index of pride, ambition, leadership and ego. Look at the back of your hand. If your first finger is much longer than your third finger, you have a strong desire to succeed. This is good, but watch that you don't push yourself too hard. If your first finger is noticeably shorter, this can suggest

a lack of confidence and you could find it hard to stand up for yourself. If the first and third fingers are roughly equal, you are reasonably ambitious but do know when to take a break and relax. The first finger should be straight. If it curves towards the second, it's a sign that going it alone isn't really your thing and you work best with the support and encouragement of others.

Second finger (Saturn finger)

Your second finger is called the Saturn finger, and it stands for responsibility and common sense. This finger should be the longest on your hand. If it is very long it suggests that you may be happiest being on your own. If it is short you may lack responsibility. You'll find that most people have Saturn fingers that are neither too short nor too long. The finger should be straight, but if it

curves towards the first or third finger
you could underrate yourself.

Third finger (Apollo finger)

Your third, or ring, finger is called your Apollo
finger. It represents creativity, self-expression and
beauty. It should be about the same length as
your first finger. If it is longer, you might have
a reckless nature. The Apollo finger should be
straight, but if it curves towards the Saturn it
suggests that this person has creative talents that
aren't being expressed, and if it curves towards
the little finger it suggests once again that you
are underrating your creative talent.

Little finger (Mercury finger)

Your little finger is called your Mercury finger, and
this is the finger that relates to communication
and how passionate you are. The average
little finger reaches up to the first joint
of the third finger (from the tip), but
the longer this finger is, the better you are at
communication. People with very short little

fingers can make wonderful communicators but it is something they have to work on. It is important for this finger to be straight, as this is a sign of honesty. When it is bent or twisted, there could be potential for dishonesty.

If you have broken a finger and it has reset in a particular way, this indicates that life is forcing you either to develop the characteristics suggested or explore new aspects of your personality.

Thumbs

Your thumb plays an important part in palmistry, and many experts believe that it clearly reveals a person's character. Thumbs contain a radial nerve that is made of the same nerve fibre that runs through our spinal columns and is found in our brains. It is this radial nerve that gives us greater reasoning abilities than other animals. Generally speaking, the larger the thumb, the greater degree of success a person can enjoy in life. People with large thumbs are often motivated, highly ambitious and have good leadership qualities. Most people have average thumbs, and this is good as it means they can stand up for themselves. People with  short thumbs can run away at the first sign of trouble or commitment, but they can also be a wonderfully calming influence on a group. If the tip of the thumb is square in shape the person will be down-to-earth, practical and have a strong sense of right and wrong. If it is shaped like a cone, the person will be graceful, charming and refined. If the tip is angled, then the person will have a busy, inventive mind.

The mounts

The mounts are areas on the palm of your hand. Mounts can be used to determine where your interests lie. A well-developed high mount shows that the person has good potential in the area indicated by the mount, whereas an underdeveloped mount shows less potential in that area. Most people's mounts are neither high nor low but flat. Have a look at your hand, and decide which mount is most prominent using the following diagram to help you.

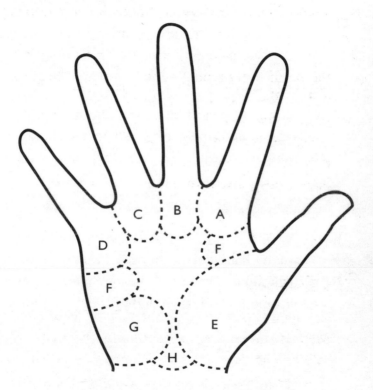

A: Mount of Jupiter
B: Mount of Saturn
C: Mount of Apollo
D: Mount of Mercury
E: Mount of Venus
F: Mounts of Mars
G: Mount of Luna
H: Mount of Neptune

If the mount is firm when pressed, this shows that you are using your abilities in that area. If it appears soft, it shows that you could explore that area more. If no mounts appear dominant, this is a sign of confidence and capability.

Mount of Jupiter

A high mount reveals someone who has good self-esteem and intelligence. When this mount is flat the person will suffer from low confidence.

Mount of Saturn

When this mount is well developed, the person will be hardworking but also a bit of a loner. If the mount is flat, it means that you can spend time on your own without feeling lonely.

Mount of Apollo

A well-developed mount shows that this person has good people skills and is easy to get along with, but there could be a desire to impress others. If the mount is flat, this is a sign of a practical, down-to-earth nature.

Mount of Mercury

People with well-developed Mercury mounts are interested in the world around them. They are

affectionate, entertaining and very agreeable. If the mount is underdeveloped, there could be insecurities and communication problems.

Mount of Venus

This mount relates to love, affection, passion and vitality. The higher the mount, the more passionate you are.

Mounts of Mars

These mounts reveal how well you can stand up for yourself. The higher the mounts, the more confidence you have.

Mount of Luna

People with well-developed Luna mounts are often creative, intuitive and imaginative. They may also be interested in mysticism and spirituality.

Mount of Neptune

A well-developed Neptune mount gives the person the ability to speak in public, come up with good ideas and make them happen.

So you see, palmistry is much more than reading lines on the palm. You can learn a great deal from a handshake and simply by looking at the size, shape, texture and fingers of the hands. You might like to write down all the positive qualities you can find in your hand and the hands of your friends in a journal. And don't forget the importance of shaking hands when you meet someone new!

CHAPTER TEN

The lines on the palm

Now we come to the part of the hand that everyone associates with palm reading – the lines on the palm. We all have four major lines: the heart, head, life and fate lines. These lines provide the bare bones of the story of our past, present and future. Palmists look at these and the way they are placed in relation to each other to gain a fuller picture. Let's start by looking at the four major lines (see the diagram over the page) and see how they interact with other lines on the hand to tell us about ourselves and our future. It is best to look at your dominant hand at this beginner stage. You should hold out your hand flat with the palm facing towards the ceiling in sunlight or in good light provided by a lamp.

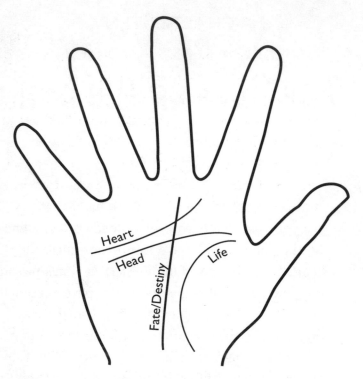

The major lines

Heart line

It's a good idea to start with the heart line, as this gives you information about a person's emotional life. The heart line is symbolic of emotion and sensitivity. The longer the heart line, the more sensitive, caring and emotional you are.

Head line

The head line signifies how intellectual, logical and headstrong you are. A head line that goes all the way across the palm reveals someone who is headstrong, dominant and driven by logic rather than emotion. It also suggests that you are a good judge of character and see things in straightforward black-and-white terms. If the head line has a downward arch, it shows that you are creative and often give other people the benefit of the doubt.

Life line

Probably the most important line of all, the life line tells you about your stamina and energy and how much you love life. It suggests how fulfilled, healthy and stable your life is likely to be. A long, thick, deep line without any breaks suggests that you have a passion and love for life and that you are energetic and likely to reach your full potential. A shorter, fainter line could indicate that you are not making the most of your skills and could try harder to achieve your goals or ambitions.

Fate line/destiny line

The fate line, or destiny line, suggests your path through life. A strong, straight fate line almost always indicates great success in your chosen career. The fate line can have branches coming off it. These relate to small ventures which you may undertake. A fate line that stops and starts in the middle of the palm could suggest lots of changes of direction. Everyone has a heart, head and life line, but not everyone has a fate line. The chances are you haven't got your fate line yet, as many people don't get them until they are in their twenties.

⋆⋆ CAN YOU DETERMINE TIMING USING THE MAJOR LINES?

Contrary to popular belief, the major lines can't predict how long your life will be, but they can suggest your potential for happiness and times of major change in your life. It takes the first thirty-five years of a person's life for the fate line to reach the head line, so don't expect yours to be very long. It takes the next fourteen years to reach

the heart line, at age forty-nine, and the rest of
the life is taken up with whatever part of the fate
line remains. It may seem bizarre that
the first thirty-five years of life take
up the bulk of the fate line, but it's
not so strange if you consider that this is the time
when we are growing up and working out what
to do with our lives. You may be surprised that
many people's fate lines stop at around forty-nine
and don't pass the heart line. This is because
many people are set in their ways at this time of
life and have settled down. People with a fate line
that carries on well beyond the heart line will
experience new and different activities in later life,
and it could be seen as a sign of long life.

The minor lines

There are a number of minor lines that you need
to look out for when reading the palm of a hand.
Generally, the fewer additional lines a person has,
the better, as most minor lines are caused by
worry and stress. That's why highly-strung people

often have hundreds of lines on their hands while their more chilled-out friends have just a few.

Unlike the major lines, minor lines can appear and disappear very quickly. If you are having a tough time with exams or have recently split up with your best friend or boyfriend, you may find a few extra marks appearing on your hands. However, as soon as the crisis is over and you feel okay again, the marks will fade and usually disappear.

Check out the opposite diagram to see where the minor lines are.

Worry lines

Most people have a series of lines that radiate from the base of their thumb towards the life line, sometimes even crossing it. These are known as worry lines, and some people have a few while others have hundreds. Most worry lines are not important, but worry lines that cross your life line could have the potential to affect your health. Most of us worry about things that never happen, so if you see lots of worry lines it might be time to relax more and enjoy life.

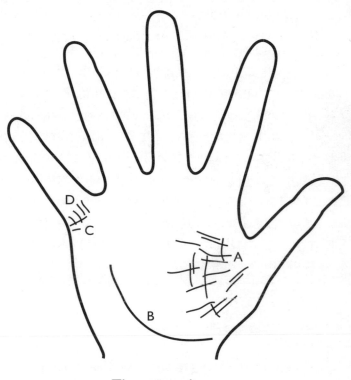

The minor lines

A: Worry lines   C: Relationship lines
B: Health lines   D: Children lines

Relationship line

If your relationship line is long and deep, it suggests a healthy and happy relationship. If there is more than one long deep line, it could mean you'll have more than one long-term relationship in your life. A shorter line could be a sign of a close friendship, and if the line is faint it could suggest that right now relationships aren't a priority for you. The closer the line is to your little finger, the later in life you will find your mate. Other important relationships can sometimes be seen on the relationship line as very small lines branching off the main line.

Children lines

The children lines are short vertical lines just beneath the little finger. Although you may see quite a few lines, it's the larger stronger lines that indicate the number of children you may have.

Health line

We don't all have a health line, but if you do the deeper the line, the greater the need for you to take care of your health. If you haven't got a health line, you are blessed with good health.

Wealth lines

Your future wealth is likely to be determined by a number of factors on your palm. Firstly, if you have a success line beneath the ring finger, you're likely to be successful and well recognized and, depending on the depth of the line, even famous! If you see branches on your life line, you could come into money through the work that you do, through marriage or even winning a competition. If you have a series of lines down the side of your palm, it may suggest a life full of travel.

Simian crease

The simian line is created when the heart line and the head line become a single line that runs across the palm. People with a simian crease have an inflexible, stubborn side to their personality, but, on the upside, they can be highly intelligent and achieve great things through sheer determination. It isn't that common to have a simian crease so it is unlikely that you will have one or see one.

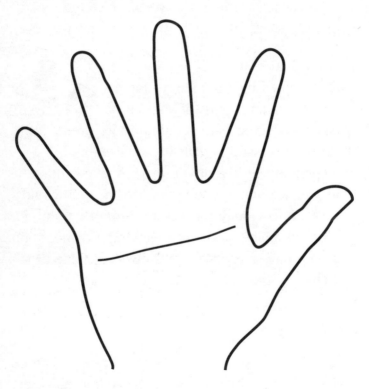

Simian crease (head and heart lines combined)

✦✦ MARKS ON THE PALM

Teacher's square

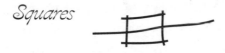

The teacher's square is made up of four lines on or just below the mount of Jupiter. It's a sign of a person who can impart knowledge to others in a way that can be easily understood. It's often found on the hands of the best teachers.

Squares

Squares that appear to protect and seal up a break in a line are called protective squares. They are a good sign, suggesting that you will find the energy to handle difficult situations. A square on a line that does not cover a break isn't such good news – it can suggest a period of conflict and lack of support.

Grilles

Grilles look like the word that describes them.
They are usually found on the mounts. They
suggest unnecessary worry and stress caused
by not thinking before you act.

Crosses

A change may be coming if a minor line crosses a
major line. But remember whether that change is
positive or negative is up to you! Crosses formed
by two minor lines are usually warning signs of
potential problems ahead.

Islands

Small ovals inside a major line suggest a series
of emotional ups and downs if they appear on the
heart line; periods of poor health if they appear
on the life line; and uncertainty and frustration
if they appear on the other lines.

Triangles

A triangle is always a positive sign and suggests that a person will find success in a creative or scientific career.

Stars

When stars are found on the mounts this is a positive sign and suggests that a person will achieve great success in the field indicated by that particular mount. However, if they are found elsewhere they can suggest a situation that gets out of control.

Dots and spots

Generally dots and spots aren't good news, as they signal blockages of energy, which could translate into poor health or emotional problems.

✴✦ YOUR LIFE IN YOUR HANDS

It's important to bear in mind when interpreting minor lines that they are, as the term suggests, minor. So don't get anxious if you see lots of dots, spots and stars. None of these marks should be interpreted on their own and need to be considered in the context of the whole hand.

 Remember too that your life really is in your hands. The lines and marks on your hands suggest likely character traits and possible outcomes, but nothing is written in stone. As mentioned earlier, as you change and grow up, so do the lines on your palms. And now that you have the basics of palmistry at your disposal, why not use that information to change your life for the better?

And don't be afraid to share your knowledge. Most of your friends will be delighted to show you their hands, and palmistry is a great way to make new friends. You can learn something from every hand that you look at, and you will have a great opportunity to help people feel good about themselves and their lives. Remember, when looking at your own as well as your friends' hands, to focus on the positive qualities and the possibilities present in each person.

To help get you started, let's take a quick look at a famous person's hands.

★★ FAMOUS HANDS

By studying the hands of famous people from photographs, you can get a sense of their true personality behind the media mask. The image of Princess Diana, for example, as expressed in her hands would appear to be in perfect contradiction to the serene, gentle, composed and somewhat fragile lady of the public image that we saw. Try to get hold of a photo showing Diana's hands to see for yourself. You'll notice that the slightly bent tip of her index finger suggests the need for support and encouragement from the public and press alike. But most revealing of all from photographs, is that the third, or ring, finger appears decidedly shorter than the first, or index, finger. This suggests that despite being cited as among the world's most attractive women, Diana never really believed she was beautiful and had no concrete idea what her direction in life should be.

Why not have a go yourself the next time you see a photo with your favourite celebrity waving or raising their hands to the camera? The press tells us one thing, but what story do their hands tell?

PART THREE

Making face and hand reading work for you

CHAPTER ELEVEN

Love and relationships

Now that you've had an introductory tour, it's time to put all that you have learnt into practice. Part three will show you just how helpful and informative face and hand reading can be in your everyday life. Let's first look at love and relationships.

A cute, sexy look doesn't really tell you anything about a person's character and how sexy they really are. Don't you want to know how that gorgeous guy you fancy is going to act in six months' time – assuming that you are still speaking? Don't you want to know what he is really like and know how compatible you might be? Face and hand readers know some pretty unexpected places to look for answers to these questions, like overlips, earlobes and little fingers.

Overlips

The overlip is not your upper lip. An overlip lies above the upper lip, forming the area between your nose tip and mouth. The technical term for this face part is philtrum. Grab a mirror and have a look at yours now. Do you see two more or less parallel raised ridges with a groove in between? Or don't you see much at all?

Your overlip structure signifies your sex appeal. If it's well defined, you are a head turner. In fact, defined overlips are extremely common among movie stars. Think Halle Berry, Kate Winslet, Cameron Diaz, Gwyneth Paltrow, Brad Pitt and Denzel Washington.

But what if your overlip isn't well defined? Does this mean you aren't powerfully attractive? Of course not. It doesn't mean that you are any less kissable either! It just means that you need to impress other people first with who you are – your kindness, sense of fun or your sporting ability.

Let's start here by telling the truth. Everyone can be sexy at times, but there are certain features that can give you clues. And you'd never guess which ones – earlobes!

Earlobes

 Check out the size of your earlobes or the earlobes of someone you really fancy. How many earrings could you fit on the earlobe? Large earlobes could hold a sizeable collection. Small earlobes have room for only one or two. Every size of earlobe is a winner with its own appeal, but generally people with larger earlobes are more physical and observant whereas those with small earlobes are more idealistic and intellectual. So if the boy you have your eye on has small earlobes, you'll impress him more with your conversation and interests than with your new haircut or outfit.

Priority areas

If you are looking for something long-term, check out your love interest's priority areas – the proportion between his forehead, nose, and chin (we met these in chapter five, see page 33). If his forehead is long, he finds ideas and communication interesting; but if it's short, your best strategy is to simply go for what you want and ask him out. If priority area two, from your eyebrows to the bottom of your nose, is dominant, this suggests an ambitious, passionate nature; and if it's small, commitment is important to him and he's more likely to be loyal. If his chin is longer than his nose or forehead, then he has a salt-of-the-earth sex appeal; and if it's small he could be endearingly impractical.

If areas one (forehead) and three (chin) are dominant, he falls in love with ideas but also has a practical side. If areas one and two (nose) are largest, expect a down-to-earth personality who is also strong on imagination. If areas two and three are largest, expect a go-getter. And if all three areas are equal, expect a really well balanced, level-headed guy.

Have you noticed that a lot of your friends or celebrities who pair off tend to look eerily similar? People with similar priority areas tend to be more compatible. Just don't take this too seriously though. You shouldn't judge anyone solely on their appearance – it takes time to get to know someone and find out whether you really are right for each other.

A real smile

How can you tell if your date is really pleased to see you? Check out his smile. If you see creases around his eyes and lowered eyebrows when you meet the chances are he's keen to see you. If you don't see a real smile straight away, though, don't give up hope – your date may be nervous and it may take a while for the genuine smile to shine through. Dimples are also worth checking out, as they are about playfulness and a sense of fun – both of which are very important when it comes to spending time with the boy you like.

★★ PUTTING IT ALL TOGETHER

Hopefully, face reading will help you find a great boy to have fun with by helping you choose dates based more on what faces show about character than what you've been considering sexy. You could even go one step further and seek out boys with face traits that relate to the qualities that matter most to you.

★★ WHAT ABOUT HAND READING?

How can palm reading help? Well, love appears in various forms in the palm. Someone with a reasonably developed mount of Venus will be very passionate. The ability to give and receive love is shown in the heart line – how clear and straight it is. A line that is too straight can suggest that the person may give more than they receive or give too much in a relationship – it takes a bit of a curve here to suggest the flexibility needed to both give and receive love. The heart line also tells you what a person likes in love, and what they look for in a boyfriend or girlfriend. The stronger and deeper the heart line, the warmer and deeper the affections; if it's wavy or broken, it can suggest fickleness.

Love relationships are much easier if the two of you have similar-shaped hands and thumbs. This is because you will think along similar lines and there will be less opportunity for conflict. It also pays to check out the little finger. Remember the longer this finger, the more passionate you are likely to be. Tension could arise if one of you has a long little finger and the other has a short one. It's also worth checking out ring (third) and index (first) finger length. If his ring finger is longer than his index finger then he probably won't think of himself as attractive. Sexiness isn't just about looks, it's also about confidence so this will really give you a clue.

And finally, don't forget that hand reading is a wonderful way to break the ice when first meeting a guy you fancy. By offering to read his hand, you can be intimate in a comfortable way. He'll love the attention, and you'll get some inside knowledge about whether he really is boyfriend material. Just remember to keep a good sense of perspective. As helpful as hand reading is, the only way to get to know a person properly is by spending time with them, chatting and sharing interests and ideas. Use what you learn from face and hand reading wisely and in conjunction with your common sense and good judgement and you can be confident that you'll make the right choice for you.

★ ★ ★ ★ ✳ ★ ⋏

CHAPTER TWELVE

Family and friends

Understanding a friend or family member better can improve your communication with that person and help you see that your point of view is only one of many possible ways of looking at something.

The information you can get from a person's face can help you avoid some conflicts and aid you in resolving others. Face reading can warn you in advance of sensitive or no-go areas. So here are some important traits to notice in your family, friends and teachers and some advice about how to avoid friction.

★★ HANDY HINTS IN FACES

 If someone you know has close-set eyes, you may be on the receiving end of their criticism. Have you ever considered the possibility that sometimes, just sometimes, they could be right?

If a friend or family member has very thin lips, respect the fact that big emotional scenes aren't their thing.

If you know someone with large front teeth, remember a big ego might be involved. You may need to stroke that ego at times. If a friend or family member has prominent canine teeth, stay out of their way! These guys are determined to win at any cost.

To avoid friction, respect the noses of your friends and family. People with scooped noses rely on their feelings; people with arched noses need to be creative; and people with straight noses like to do things their way. Admire the efforts of your short-nosed friend, but don't take her for granted; and don't forget that your long-nosed brother or sister needs to feel that they are making an important contribution.

Remember that people with starter eyebrows (thicker in the middle, towards the nose) don't like to be given too much responsibility, but ender eyebrows (thicker on the outside) do. Starters have lots of creativity and enthusiasm, so make sure you invite them to your parties. But for help with your homework you might like to ask an ender.

If a friend has a great deal of asymmetry or lopsidedness in their face, you could be in for a lot of complications. She's independent and fun but wacky and wild at times too, and she might do things that unintentionally hurt others.

If you reread the information about cheeks (see pages 23–24), you'll recall that people with prominent cheeks like to be the centre of attention and there could be a lot of intensity in your friendship.

If your Mum, Dad, sister or friend has high cheekbones, watch out. If they catch you living a lie, you might see facial expressions and hear words you never imagined!

 Watch out if you know someone with a very angled chin. Acknowledge their powerful need to stay in control, and give them lots of leeway.

Your friend's eyelid proportions can change faster than you think. All it takes is one late night or a good cry. So check them out on a daily basis and use your eyelid awareness to better understand what your friend is going through.

When eyes angle up towards the side of the face, this suggests an optimistic, idealistic nature. Such eyes come with high expectations for a child, friend, brother or sister. If eyes angle down towards the nose, this is the problem finder and solver, so don't be surprised if this person is always foreseeing potential problems and putting the dampers on things. And if you know someone with even eyes, expect a good dose of realism but also moodiness and intolerance when things don't go their way.

Remember to watch a person's mouth when it is at rest to see how they interpret what others say. If you pass your friend in a hurry with a seemingly innocent comment such as, 'Can't stop now I'm in a rush!', will she be sure you are rushing to something wonderful and be glad you let her know (the upturned mouth)? Will she feel hurt and neglected (the downward mouth)? Or will she just wonder why you're in such a hurry (the even mouth)?

You can learn something from everyone, but do bear in mind that, like it or not, family members will share similar features and traits. In the words of the writer, Gail Buckley, 'Family faces are magic mirrors. Looking at people who belong to us, we see our present, past and future. We make discoveries about ourselves.'

★ ★ ★ ★ ✳ ★ ★ ★

⋆⋆ HANDY HINTS IN HANDS

As for hands, watch out for hand gestures.
Remember the less you see the hands move,
the more likely it is that someone you know is
holding back or, in the worst case scenario, lying.
It doesn't have to be wild hand gestures, tiny
movements will do, but generally it's a good
sign to see the voice accompanied in some way
by the hands.

Check out the life line when it comes to
relationships with family and friends. It shows
how settled you feel and how much you are
enjoying your life. You may notice that the line is
stronger in places than others. The faint places
suggest times of conflict or stress. If those faint
places appear at or near the beginning of the life
line above the thumb, you could be feeling
stressed by the situation at home or your
friendships could be difficult. If this is the case,
acknowledge the problem and deal with it.

Sometimes it's easier to stick your
head in the sand, but if you don't
acknowledge that something is
bothering you, it will never change. If

you can do something to change the situation –
for example, make new friends or tidy up your
room when Mum asks you to – then do it. If you
feel there is nothing you can do – for example,
your parents are divorcing or you are being bullied
at school – ask for help from a grown-up you can
trust, or phone a helpline. Above all, don't ignore
the problem and hope it will go away. Use the
information you're gaining about yourself and
others to help you do something about it instead.

Are you feeling confident of your abilities as a
face and hand reader? You should be familiar with
the meanings of different features and be able to
impress your friends and family with your new
talents. The more you practise the better you'll get
– so have some fun with your friends and see
what you can find out about each other.

CHAPTER THIRTEEN

School, money, work and health

School

When it comes to your attitude towards school, look no further than your nose. If you have a straight nose, you are more likely to work hard and efficiently and the teachers will love you. Just be careful, though, that your disciplined approach doesn't lead to a lack of tolerance for others less able to cope than you are.

People with scooped noses work hard and are academic too, but they are very vulnerable to criticism. If this is you, do make sure you take regular time out and don't become obsessed by your work. When you get feedback from teachers, try to

stand back a bit and don't overreact. It
isn't the end of the world if you didn't do
as well as you know you could. Just take
a deep breath, learn from your mistakes and
try again.

If your nose is arched or curved, you have a
real creative talent. The only trouble is that you
are so creative you may not pay attention to the
important details that you need to succeed. Your
work also goes in fits and starts, and your biggest
challenge is to try to be more consistent.

Whether your fingers are long or short can
also indicate your approach to schoolwork. If you

have short fingers, your enthusiasm is
commendable but your main challenge is
to work on staying power and completing
what you have started. If you have long
fingers, you finish tasks from beginning to end
to the best of your ability, but watch out that you
don't get so lost in the detail that you fall behind.
And finally, if your fingers are neither long nor
short, you are a wonderful mix of patience,
impatience, discipline and slapdash.
Your challenge is to keep everything
on an even keel.

Money

Your nose can also tell you a lot about your spending style. Remember that, in general, the larger the nostrils, the more you like to spend money on yourself and others. If this is you, remember that money problems are often a part of life, but you can make your life a lot less stressful by spending less than you earn.

Money is indicated on the hand in three ways. Inherited money is shown by a small line between the third and fourth finger that curves part of the way around the third finger. Unfortunately, it doesn't show how much or when  this money will be inherited. Little triangles on the inside of the life line could suggest easy money, such as a Lotto win, but most people have to earn their money, and that is indicated by the thumb. If the second part of the thumb is longer than the tip section, the person will be more of a thinker than a money-maker. You also need to look at the head line on your palm. A short head line often suggests a highly shrewd thinker, and

someone like this could make a lot of money.
Just remember that palm reading about money
only indicates potential and it is up to you how
to achieve it.

Future career

You may find that face and hand reading can help
you make decisions about your future choice of
career. Hopefully you've had a few 'aha' moments
when reading this book, when you thought, 'Yes,
that's me!' Connecting your unique talents to
your facial features or the lines on your hand can
give you the self-confidence and self-knowledge
you need to think and plan ahead. For example, if
you need to be creative, or if you have an eye for
detail, or if you are the kind of person who likes
to be the centre of attention, you can now start
to look at career options that make the most of
those qualities. The future is yours to shape –
what do you want to do?

Health

Remember your face type back in Part one (see pages 13–16)? Well, it can give you some pretty useful information about your health. If you're a wood type, you can be prone to headaches and stomach upsets, and it's important for you to reduce stress, which can make these problems worse. Make sure you eat healthily and give yourself enough time to relax and get plenty of fresh air to clear your head.

If you are a fire type, you may be prone to anxiety and skin problems. It's crucial for you to enjoy friendships with a wide range of people but also to be able to learn how to relax on your own. Coffee, fizzy drinks and spicy food can make anxiety worse, so try to avoid them when you're feeling stressed.

If you are an earth type, you are, like wood types, more likely to get headaches and stomach problems, and you need to learn to find ways to

103

calm yourself so worry doesn't make
things worse. Avoid a diet that is too
high in sugar and dairy products, and
steer clear of large meals late at night.

If you are a metal type, you could be susceptible
to frequent colds and flu. Breathing properly is
important for you, and you could benefit from
regular daily exercise. Watch out for junk food,
spicy food and too much milk, as they can give
you stomach upsets.

If you are a water type, you are prone to
tiredness, so avoid overworking on school projects
or hobbies and try to find ways to relax.
Stimulants such as tea, coffee and fizzy drinks
give you a short boost but add to feelings of
stress and anxiety, so these should be avoided.

Your hands can also give you clues as to your
physical health. People with broader hands
tend to have more energy and enjoy better
health than those with narrow hands. The
number of lines on a hand is also a clue. This is
because many lines are caused by stress and

nervous tension, and both of these can make you feel unwell. The life line can also be a good indicator of health. Ideally it should be clear, well-marked and reach across the palm. A large mount of Venus gives vitality and energy, which have an enormous effect on your health.

Remember to use your common sense and keep a good sense of perspective. If you are worried about your health, or just don't feel so good, the first step is to seek advice from your doctor, the school nurse or an adult you can trust. But if you eat a healthy, balanced diet and exercise regularly you should be in good health and be well equipped to deal with whatever the future holds.

CHAPTER FOURTEEN

Happiness

Some people seem to be happy most of the time, whatever happens to them, whereas others seem to enjoy feeling miserable. It is sometimes possible to determine who these people are by looking at their hands and their faces.

 For happiness, look at the quality of the life line on the palm, which is related to the person's energy levels, and also how broad their hand is. If the person has a broad hand and a well-marked life line, the chances are they are an optimist. You also need to look at the head line to see if the person is using their head. People with questioning minds have the potential for great happiness because they are always learning something new.

People who are nervous and tense tend to be less happy than those who are calmer. Therefore, people with fewer lines on their hands are generally happier than those with a network of tension on theirs. Fortunately, though, we all have the power to change. Believe it or not, happiness is a choice. You can choose to be happy and to make the best of things. This choice has to come from within, though – and remember, it takes time and effort to make happiness a habit. One of the great things about palm reading is that if you act on positive suggestions it will, in time, be made visible in your palms.

Your face too may change in subtle ways as you settle into adulthood, but certain things, such as the shape of your eyes or your nose, are not likely to change that much. What you can change, however, is the way that you feel about your face, and this is perhaps the single most powerful and helpful thing you can do.

✦✦ PRETTY OR PLAIN?
IT DOESN'T MATTER!

You've seen how your face is a reflection of the inner you. Every trait means something about who you are inside. You are, in fact, loaded with unique talents that make you one of a kind. It doesn't matter whether you consider yourself pretty or plain; from the perspective of face reading everyone is a winner. That's why face reading is so great for building your self-esteem.

Let's start with beauty. Attractive people always seem to have a head start when it comes to love, friendship and work options.

But here's something interesting to consider. Psychologists at the University of Texas and Arkansas have made a shocking discovery. What we really admire about pretty faces is how evenly proportioned their features are. Facial symmetry – seen in film stars like Halle Berry and Jude Law – is often thought of as a key factor in attractiveness. As a face reader you can appreciate what it means to have an

108

average face. It simply means your
personality strikes a happy medium
between two extremes. You fit in
well everywhere, but it can be hard
for you to find a distinctive talent other than the
ability to look good.

There's something else you should know about
beauty. Beautiful people don't always have

 average, even features. Something about
them makes them stand out – be it an
out-of-proportion nose, huge eyes or
overlarge lips. It's often irregular features
that signal talent and charisma. Think of
Madonna's gappy teeth, Nicole Kidman's tiny nose
and Britney's high forehead. Basically, the more
unique your features, the greater the chance you
have of being a true individual capable of making
your own special mark on the world.

Right now in your life, standing out may not
be your chief concern. Hanging out with the
crowd and blending in may be what you long for.
Just bear in mind, though, that the
popular crowd with the even, average
looks aren't always the ones with the
greatest skills or talents, or the ones

who are necessarily going to go on to do great
things with their lives.

The happiest and most beautiful people
aren't always the ones who fit in but the
ones who have the courage to be themselves.
Gwyneth Paltrow, who has a face that is
beautiful but not at all symmetrical, put it well
when she said, 'Beauty to me is being comfortable
in your own skin.' So love and appreciate your
face and the unique talents it reflects. And see
the beauty in other people too.

Find the courage to see the face and the
talents that are there. No feature, however pretty
or striking, is exempt from the challenges and
lessons of life. Understand that being different
isn't wrong but wonderful. Faces are about so
much more than prettiness, and there is so much
more to you or anyone you see than meets the
eye. There is no one standard for what looks right.
So from now on, don't just look at a face – look
into it.

AFTERWORD

Amazing you

Face and hand reading can help build your self-esteem by showing you that there is so much about you that is unique. Best of all, though, face and hand reading can help you understand others and yourself much more.

 Understanding other people can help you see other people's points of view and get on with them better. Understanding yourself can stop you from feeling that you have zero control over your life. You may not think much about self-awareness, but it is essential. If you don't know yourself, you can be swayed by what others think you should be, think and do. That can interfere with your ability to make smart decisions and do what you want with your life. But when you are armed with self-knowledge, you can feel optimistic about your future and feel more in control because you know that within you is the power to turn things around.

You are far more powerful than you think you are. Take the time to learn about yourself, and you'll soon discover that you're amazing. Believe in yourself, be who you are, and don't ever put yourself down in comparison to other people. The secrets in your face and hands show you that you have the potential for an incredible life. Now it is up to YOU to live it.

Index

✴ ✴